POPULAR CULTURE

A VIEW FROM THE PAPARAZZI

Orlando Bloom	John Legend
Kelly Clarkson	Lindsay Lohan
Johnny Depp	Mandy Moore
Hilary Duff	Ashlee and Jessica Simpson
Will Ferrell	
Jake Gyllenhaal	Justin Timberlake
Paris and Nicky Hilton	Owen and Luke Wilson
LeBron James	Tiger Woods

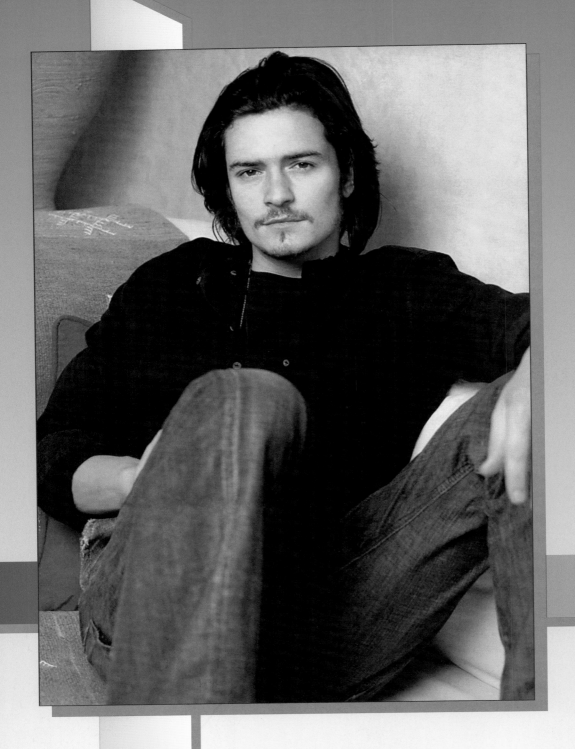

Orlando Bloom

Joanne Mattern

Mason Crest Publishers

Orlando Bloom

FRONTIS
British actor Orlando Bloom has proven that he is more than just another good-looking face with a series of starring roles in blockbuster movies.

Produced by 21st Century Publishing and Communications, Inc.

MASON CREST PUBLISHERS INC.
370 Reed Road
Broomall, Pennsylvania 19008
(866) MCP-BOOK (toll free)
www.masoncrest.com

Printed in the United States.

First Printing

9 8 7 6 5 4 3 2 1

Library of Congress Cataloging-in-Publication Data

Mattern, Joanne, 1963–
    Orlando Bloom / Joanne Mattern.
        p. cm. — (Pop culture: a view from the paparazzi)
    Includes bibliographical references and index.
    Hardback edition: ISBN-13: 978-1-4222-0198-5
    Paperback edition: ISBN-13: 978-1-4222-0352-1
    1. Bloom, Orlando, 1977–   —Juvenile literature.   2. Motion picture actors and actresses—Great Britain—Biography—Juvenile literature.   I. Title.
PN2598.B6394M38 2008
791.4302'8092—dc22
[B]   2007018484

CONTENTS

Orlando Bloom drew praise from his costars, as well as from movie fans, for his portrayal of Will Turner, one of the heroes of Disney's *Pirates of the Caribbean* series of films. "Orlando's enormously talented, but he's also made some really smart choices," says Jerry Bruckheimer, who produced the three hit *Pirates* films.

1

Success Blooms!

In the summer of 2006, many people were anxious to see *Pirates of the Caribbean: Dead Man's Chest*, the sequel to the 2003 hit *Pirates of the Caribbean: The Curse of the Black Pearl*. When *Dead Man's Chest* proved to be a huge success as well, it launched one of its stars, Orlando Bloom, into the record books.

The original *Pirates* film, in which Bloom played blacksmith-turned-pirate Will Turner, had **grossed** more than $650 million worldwide and left audiences calling for more. In *The Curse of the Black Pearl*, Will Turner must rescue his love, Elizabeth Swann (played by Keira Knightley), who has been taken prisoner by pirates on a cursed ship, the *Black Pearl*. The pirates mistakenly believe

The romantic relationship between Elizabeth Swann (Keira Knightley) and Will Turner appeals to many *Pirates of the Caribbean* fans. Keira explained Orlando's appeal to young girls by jokingly calling him a "one-man boy band," but she fueled teen magazine speculations about the young actor by saying, "I can report that he's a very good kisser."

that Elizabeth is the only person who can set them free from the curse. To save Elizabeth, Will enlists the help of a pirate named Jack Sparrow (played by Johnny Depp). Jack has his own reason for helping—he wants to take command of the *Black Pearl*—and the two characters have a hard time trusting each other. In the end, however, the two are able to rescue Elizabeth and to escape jail and execution.

To many people's surprise, *Pirates of the Caribbean: The Curse of the Black Pearl* was as popular with critics as it was with audiences. The film was nominated for several Academy Awards, including Best Makeup, Best Sound, Best Sound Editing, and Best Visual Effects. In addition, Johnny Depp was nominated for Best Actor.

Coming Back for More

As the second movie in Disney's *Pirates* **trilogy**, the 2006 sequel *Pirates of the Caribbean: Dead Man's Chest* was even more successful than the first movie had been. *Dead Man's Chest* earned more than $135 million on its opening weekend, easily beating the previous record for first-weekend earnings by a movie (*Spider-Man*, with $114.8 million). All of the most popular characters were back for *Dead Man's Chest*,

Will Turner, shown in a swordfight during *Dead Man's Chest*, has changed since the first film. "I sort of indicated I'd like Will to develop into a more dynamic pirate as opposed to being more of a straight-laced . . . stick-in-the-mud," Orlando told the *Toronto Star*. "I wanted him to . . . maybe have a few darker edges."

including Depp's spastic Captain Jack Sparrow and Orlando's clever and passionate Will Turner. Orlando praised the writers and crew that made the second film possible:

> **"What's cool about it is that the talent, the writers, . . . took what was a one-off movie, but because of what was already there on the page in terms of character-development, they were able to really take it somewhere."**

While the two lead characters had been friends in the first movie, *Dead Man's Chest* saw them turning on one another like never before. They faced deadly cannibals, the vicious Davy Jones, and the monstrous Kraken on their journey to save Jack's soul and free Will from execution at the hands of the East India Company. Will needed Jack's compass to bribe the company into setting him free, while Jack needed the key to the chest containing Davy Jones's heart. Both Will and Jack proved willing to sacrifice the other if necessary. Also returning in the film was Keira Knightly as Elizabeth, while Jack Davenport played the disgraced Commodore Norrington. Elizabeth was instrumental in finding the chest, but it was ultimately Norrington who stole Davy Jones's heart and returned it to the East India Company, hoping to regain his post as commodore. At the end of the movie, Jack was dragged under the waves by the Kraken, and Will's fate was uncertain.

Even though critics complained that *Dead Man's Chest* was too long and had an overly complicated plot, viewers still flooded the theaters. The movie was the number one film of the summer and quickly became the most popular movie of the year. By the time *Dead Man's Chest* had finished its run in theaters, it had earned more than a billion dollars.

Setting a Record

This was not the first time Orlando Bloom had appeared in a movie that had earned more than a billion dollars. Many movie fans already knew him as the blond, statuesque elf hero Legolas in the three *Lord of the Rings* movies. Legolas was his breakout role, as *The Lord of the Rings* trilogy drew huge audiences. The first movie, *The Fellowship of the Ring*, grossed $871 million. The second film, *The Two Towers*,

As Legolas the elf (center) in the *Lord of the Rings* trilogy of films, Orlando Bloom emerged as a star with a huge following. Combined, the three movies earned nearly $3 billion at the box office. Orlando is just the second actor to appear in more than one movie that grossed more than a billion dollars.

Orlando has emerged as one of Hollywood's most popular young celebrities in part because of his appeal to girls and women. However, the modest actor generally tries to downplay his teen idol status. "I don't really let the sex-symbol thing be a part of my consciousness," he told *People* in 2005.

brought in $926 million, and the final installment, *The Return of the King*, capped off the success of the franchise with a worldwide gross of $1.1 billion. *The Return of the King* also won the 2004 Academy Award for Best Picture.

The success of *Pirates of the Caribbean: Dead Man's Chest* meant that Orlando was only the second actor to ever appear in more than one movie that had grossed over a billion dollars. The first actor to do this was Bernard Hill, who had appeared in *The Return of the King* and the hit movie *Titanic*. But Hill's roles in these films were relatively small, while Orlando was a star in both of his hit movies.

Orlando clearly has star power. His good looks and charismatic manners have made him a household name. According to biographer Jonathan Carlisle:

> **"With a face that could melt a million hearts, Orlando has taken both Hollywood and the movie-going public by storm. His combination of gorgeous good looks and blazing talent has made him the hottest performer in Tinseltown, appealing to fans and casting directors alike. Which makes it no surprise that his career has taken a meteoric path."**

But Orlando Bloom did not enter the acting business to be just a famous face. He has wanted to act since he was very little. And for him, this meant meeting the **challenges** of playing different characters, not becoming a typical Hollywood star.

Watching actors on television, in movies, and on the stage inspired Orlando to choose acting as a career. "When I realized the heroes on *The A-Team* and *Knight Rider* weren't real, I decided I wanted to act because I thought, 'I'd love to be any number of those guys,'" Orlando admitted to *Teen People* in 2004.

2

A Young Adventurer

Orlando Jonathan Blanchard Bloom was born on January 13, 1977, in Canterbury, a city in southern England. He came from an interesting and intellectual family. His mother, Sonia Copeland Bloom, ran a school that taught English to foreign students. And his father, Harry Bloom, who was many years older than Sonia, was once a lawyer in **apartheid** South Africa.

A Fight Against Injustice

During the time when Harry lived in South Africa, the nation was torn apart by a system called apartheid. Under apartheid, black Africans were treated like second-class citizens. They had few legal rights and were often abused by the white ruling minority of the country.

Harry Bloom devoted much of his life to fighting apartheid inside and outside the courtroom. In 1956 he wrote a novel called *Transvaal Episode* that described a racial uprising in a South African town. Government leaders were so alarmed by the book that they banned it. Harry Bloom also spent time working with other activists, including Nelson Mandela, the famous anti-apartheid movement leader who spent 27 years in prison for sabotage.

As he got older, Harry decided he wanted a quieter life. In 1963 he and Sonia moved to England, where Harry became a professor of law at the University of Kent in Canterbury. Their daughter, Samantha, was born in 1975. Orlando followed in 1977.

Family Life

Many people have wondered where Orlando's unusual name came from. It was chosen for two reasons. The first was that both Sonia and Harry loved the works of a 17th-century music composer named Orlando Gibbons. The second was that, as Sonia later explained, "Harry had trouble with his students' names and thought he would always remember an Orlando."

Orlando never really got to know his father. On July 28, 1981, when Orlando was only four years old, Harry died. Because he was so young, Orlando does not have many lasting memories of his father. However, Sonia and other family members made sure both Orlando and Samantha knew what Harry had been like and understood the things he had believed in. Orlando later said:

"My mother has always spoken highly of him. He's been a role model for me in my head. Harry was a great man. It was as though he'd done his job and left the world."

After Harry died, a close family friend named Colin Stone was appointed as guardian for both children. He would care for them if anything happened to their mother. Colin was so close to the family that he even lived with them for a time.

A Love of the Arts

Although Colin Stone was an important part of the Bloom children's lives, Sonia was the one who had the most influence on Orlando and Samantha. She loved literature, the performing arts, and music, and she made sure her children had plenty of opportunities to express themselves through the arts. According to Orlando:

Orlando maintains close relationships with members of his family. In this photo, taken at the London premiere of *Kingdom of Heaven* in May 2005, the actor is joined by his mother Sonia (left), his grandmother Betty (second from left), and his sister Samantha (right), who is two years older than Orlando.

> "My mother was quite interested in both my sister and me being creative. She was always taking us to the theatre to see plays and musicals, and she'd do things like enter us into the Canterbury Festival [a local fair], which was good because it got both of us used to being in front of an audience."

Sonia gave her children more than a good education and a love of the arts. She also gave them a sense of adventure. She was a firm believer in having new experiences. Because of her attitude and Harry Bloom's dedication to ending injustice, Orlando always believed that taking risks was an important part of life.

Schoolboy Adventures

As part of his education, young Orlando attended local private schools. However, Orlando struggled in the classroom because he has a mild form of the learning disorder dyslexia. People with dyslexia often invert letters and numbers, and sometimes have trouble recognizing letters and numbers and associating them with the proper sounds. It is hard for them to read and make sense of words. Through his own hard work, and with the help of his mother and teachers, Orlando was able to overcome his learning problems. He had to work harder than the other kids, but he passed his exams regardless.

It became obvious early on that Orlando had a taste for danger. He enjoyed sports, and even as a child, he was not afraid to take risks. Orlando admitted as much himself:

> "I was a little bit crazy. Not crazy-crazy, but I was always the first one to jump off the wall or dive into the lake, without really thinking about the consequences of my actions."

His daring often led to injuries. When he was nine years old, Orlando broke his leg while on a ski trip. He spent the next few months laying on the couch, eating junk food, and feeling sorry for himself. But as soon as his leg healed, he jumped right back into action.

Throughout all his adventures, Orlando remained fascinated by acting. He identified with the characters he saw in movies, television shows, and plays. He was also a big fan of the Superman comics and the 1978 *Superman* movie, starring Christopher Reeve. He once explained:

> **The reason I got into acting was because when I was younger, I had an incredible imagination, like most kids, and I was always drawn to these larger-than-life characters that I would see either at the theatre, on TV or at the cinema. Once I was old enough to realise that those characters weren't real, they were actors—once I realised I could be Superman—I was like, 'Man, I can become an actor and be all of those things.'**

A Shocking Surprise

By the time he was 13 years old, Orlando was growing into a confident and outgoing young man. He was secure about his family and his life. But that security was disrupted a bit when Sonia had a serious talk with her children during a family vacation. Sonia explained that even though she had been married to Harry Bloom when Samantha and Orlando were born, Harry was not their biological father. Their father was actually Colin Stone, the Bloom children's legal guardian.

Orlando was shocked by the news, and to this day he has spoken very little about it to the press. However, he has made it clear that he did not feel betrayed or unloved. He once said:

> **It's an unusual story, but then, you show me a family and I'll show you an unusual story. I was really lucky. I had two dads.**

A Move to London

When he was in his teens, Orlando appeared in a number of local theater productions. At age 16, he took his final school examinations. He passed them all but got the best grades in theater, sculpture, and art. It seemed clear what Orlando was meant to do. With the encouragement of his mother and other family members, the young man made a big decision. He would leave home and attend a drama school in London.

The London theater community was quick to recognize Orlando's talent and determination. He won a scholarship to the National Youth Theatre, one of England's best companies for young actors. Many

When he was 13 years old Orlando was surprised to learn that Colin Stone, not Harry Bloom, was his biological father. Colin had served as legal guardian to Samantha and Orlando after Harry's death. Here, Colin and Orlando pose for a photograph at the October 2005 premiere of *Elizabethtown* in New York.

famous British actors have studied there, including Ben Kingsley, Derek Jacobi, Helen Mirren, and Daniel Day-Lewis. The National Youth Theatre's artistic director, Ed Wilson, would later call Orlando "one of the finest young performers we've ever had in our companies."

Although for the next few years Orlando was busy studying at the National Youth Theatre and working to pay his bills, he still found time to have fun. He began to hang out with an older crowd and enjoyed going to dance clubs and parties. He also enjoyed shopping, even though he could not always afford the high-fashion items he wanted.

Becoming an Actor

In 1995 Orlando took on a new challenge. He was offered a one-year scholarship to the British American Drama Academy, also known as BADA. Soon after he started at BADA, he appeared in a play in north London. There was an **agent** in the audience who liked what she saw. She agreed to represent Orlando and find acting jobs for him. Soon Orlando was hired to appear in a small part on the British television series *Casualty*.

His next offer was even more exciting—a role in a motion picture! The film was called *Wilde*, and it was a biography of the controversial Irish writer Oscar Wilde, who had lived in the late 1800s. Orlando's part was very small, as he had just one line.

Although the young actor enjoyed the experience of making *Wilde*, he did not feel he was ready to jump into larger film roles yet. Instead, he wanted to stay in school and learn how to be an actor before he made that leap. He told reporters:

> **"I always planned to go to drama school. I suppose I could have trained in the industry more. But, instead, I chose an environment that would be more conducive to experimenting."**

The environment Orlando chose was the Guildhall School of Music and Drama in London. He loved his time there. He was able to take on a number of different roles in plays at the school, including parts in the ancient Greek plays *Antigone* and *Troiades* (*The Trojan Women*), Anton Chekhov's classic *The Seagull*, and a teleplay called *A Night Out* which had been written in the 1960s. Orlando appreciated the freedom to play so many different parts, and enjoyed being able to experiment in the safety of a school. He later explained:

> **"That's probably what kept me sound in the head, getting the chance to mess it up in the safety of an environment where it's all about education and growing and learning."**

Orlando's acting days might have ended after a 1998 fall that left him with a broken back. Although doctors felt that he might not walk again, the young actor was able to recover fairly quickly. Orlando still enjoys such adventurous hobbies as skydiving and bungee jumping, but today admits being "more cautious. I've accepted that I'm not invincible."

Crashing Down

Orlando's life and career almost ended one Sunday afternoon in the spring of 1998. He was visiting friends in a London apartment, and the group decided to go up onto the roof of the building. They found that the door to the roof was stuck, so Orlando crawled out of a window and tried to climb up a drainpipe to reach the roof and kick the door open. His weight was too much for the pipe, and it broke away from the building. Orlando fell three floors to the concrete courtyard below.

He was rushed to the hospital, and the news was not good. He had broken three bones in his back and three ribs. He had also bruised his spinal cord. Doctors told the young actor that he would never walk again.

Orlando and his family were devastated by the news. The young man had always been physically active, and he couldn't bear the news that he was paralyzed. He later told reporters:

> **"I experienced all these weird moments where I was exploring really dark corners of my mind. I was lying there on my back, unable to do anything. You don't know how you're going to be under those circumstances. It was the biggest test of my life."**

Then the doctors offered him hope. There was an operation that might help him to walk again, but it was risky. Orlando chose to take the risk. Surgeons cut open his back and bolted metal plates to his spine. Twelve days later, he limped out of the hospital to continue his recovery at home.

Orlando had to wear a back brace for a year. He also had to do difficult exercises and learn to walk again. His hard work paid off, though. By the end of the year, he was back at school and back on stage.

Orlando's accident changed him forever. He realized that he could not just jump into things and that his actions could have serious consequences. Although he was able to go back to sports and other physical activities, Orlando's back still hurts if he overdoes things. He has said that he welcomes the back pain, however, because it is a constant reminder of how lucky he is.

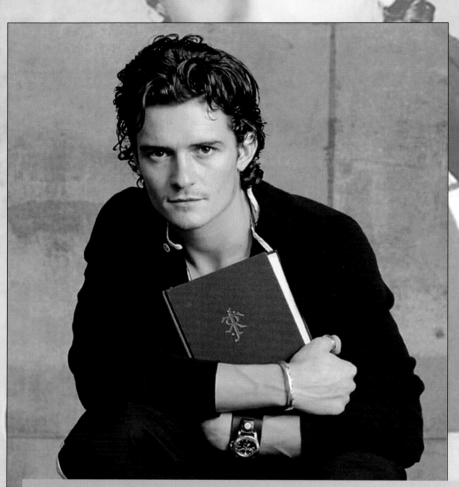

Orlando poses with a copy of J.R.R. Tolkien's master-piece *The Lord of the Rings*. Tolken's trilogy of fantasy novels about an apocalyptic struggle between the forces of good and evil are among the most popular works of modern literature. Orlando was thrilled to be offered a major part in the movies.

3

Lord of
the Elves

B y early 1999 Orlando was back at school and back at work. He planned to continue his studies and aim for a career as a stage actor, but fate intervened. A massive project was underway in Australia to bring the beloved *Lord of the Rings* books to the big screen, and Orlando had an opportunity to be part of it.

Bad News and Great News

In 1999 director Peter Jackson held **auditions** for a three-movie project called *The Lord of the Rings*. The movies were based on a trilogy of fantasy novels that had been written by British author J.R.R. Tolkien. The novels follow the journey of a **mythical** creature called a hobbit as he journeys to destroy a powerful gold ring in a volcano. The ring must be destroyed so that it will not fall into the hands of an evil creature named Sauron, who wants to use its power to take over the world. Frodo, the hobbit, is joined on his journey by other hobbits, humans, elves, a wizard, and an irritable dwarf, and the fate of the world is in their hands.

Tolkien's books were widely considered classics, and had influenced several generations of readers and fantasy writers around the world. The pressure was on Peter Jackson to make movies that would remain true to Tolkien's story, yet seem fresh, new, and thrilling for audiences to watch. The project was an enormous undertaking, and everything had to be just right. Jackson looked at hundreds of actors for the 15 major roles in the films. Taking his agent's advice, Orlando sent in an audition tape, hoping to get the part of Faramir, a warrior who helps the hobbits.

A few months after his audition, Orlando received news. Another actor had been chosen to play Faramir. But there was more—Jackson had been impressed by the young actor's talent, and wanted Orlando to play a much bigger part. The director thought the young man's high cheekbones, handsome features, and slender, athletic body were perfect for the character of Legolas, an elf. Jackson later recalled:

> **❝The first time we saw Orlando, we rewound the tape, looked at him again, and then looked at each other. He was straight out of drama school, but we knew we'd struck gold.❞**

Orlando was stunned. Legolas was a major character who would appear in all three movies. He read Tolkien's books again and made another audition tape, this time as the elf. The producers liked what they saw, and Orlando was offered the movie deal. Two days later, he graduated from Guildhall.

Getting Ready

In *The Lord of the Rings*, Legolas is an elven warrior who has been alive for more than 2,900 years. His age and experience make him calm and fearless in the face of even the most horrible evil. Orlando worked to put himself in Legolas's mind, so he could understand why

The New Zealand filmmaker Peter Jackson was virtually unknown in the United States when he gained the rights to direct a film version of *The Lord of the Rings* in 1997. Jackson decided to film all three movies at the same time, so Orlando and the other actors spent 18 months filming scenes for the trilogy.

the character behaves the way he does. Legolas is a fighter, but he never loses his temper. He is determined, quiet, and steady.

Orlando had to get comfortable with the physical aspects of his character. He practiced walking silently and stealthily, like a cat. Orlando explained:

"You know how cats can jump and land steadily on their paws? That's what I'm trying to do. There's a strength in that, but it's very balletic. It's also bloody hard to do without falling over!"

There were a variety of physical skills necessary for the role. The young actor was required to ride horses, although this was no problem, as he had been riding since he was a child. However, Legolas is an

"It was like winning the lottery," Orlando said of being cast as Legolas. "I mean, imagine being flown to this amazing country and being taught how to shoot a bow and arrow, learn to ride horses and study swordplay! I was pinching myself. Not until I'd filmed a few scenes did I finally believe it was actually happening."

Aragorn (Viggo Mortensen), Legolas (Orlando), and Gandalf (Sir Ian McKellen) pause on horseback in a scene from *The Two Towers*. "I did some pretty wicked stuff on horseback," Orlando later told an interviewer. "It really was insane what I had to do, but it was so much fun and I had real faith in my horse."

expert archer, so Orlando had to learn to shoot a bow and arrow while he rode. Sword fighting classes he had taken in drama school also came in handy.

Playing Legolas presented Orlando with another challenge as well. Tolkien had made up an elvish language for his characters, and any actor playing an elf would need to learn how to speak it. Orlando found grasping elvish quite difficult, but Jackson provided several experts to make sure he could speak the language fluently by the time filming began.

Off to New Zealand

Making the *Lord of the Rings* trilogy would be very expensive because of the high cost of special effects and computer-generated characters. In order to keep costs down, Jackson decided to film all three *Lord of the Rings* movies at the same time. Movies are rarely shot this way, because no one knows if a film will be popular enough to warrant a sequel. Orlando and the other actors had to move to New Zealand for 18 months to complete the project.

Orlando found himself surrounded by an amazingly talented group of actors. A young American named Elijah Wood played Frodo the Hobbit. Wood had been a child star and had already appeared in a number of movies. Other members of the cast included Cate Blanchett, Liv Tyler, Sean Astin, Viggo Mortensen, and veteran horror movie actor Christopher Lee. Two of England's most **acclaimed** actors, Sir Ian Holm and Sir Ian McKellen, also had major roles in the films.

At first, Orlando was nervous about working with such distinguished and talented actors. He had only just graduated from drama school, and his movie experience amounted to one minor part in a small movie. He decided to learn all he could from his costars and get the most out of the experience.

The cast members quickly became good friends. Orlando developed an especially friendly relationship with Viggo Mortensen, who played the hero Aragorn. The two often teased each other. Orlando described a typical exchange:

> **"Vig used to call me 'elf boy' and I'd call him 'filthy human.' As an Elf, I never got a scratch on me, never got dirty. And Vig would come out with blood and sweat all over him. And he'd say to me, 'Oh, go manicure your nails.'"**

In celebration of the bond they formed over those 18 months, Orlando and his costars got identical tattoos. The tattoo reads "Nine," which is a reference to the nine adventurers who band together in the story. The cast was also given rings by the crew inscribed with the elvish words meaning "Wherever it May Lead."

During the long period making the *Lord of the Rings* films, Orlando and his costars developed a close bond. The members of the cast each got tattoos of the Elvish word for "nine." Orlando had a particularly good friendship with Viggo Mortensen, the American actor who played Aragorn in the three films.

Reality and Moving On

Orlando had a serious girlfriend during the time he filmed the *Rings* trilogy. The British woman's identity has never been revealed, but she visited him in New Zealand and even lived there for several months. However, the couple found it difficult to maintain their relationship when they were so far apart. Shortly before the trilogy finished filming, they broke up. Although Orlando has never talked much about this relationship, he has discussed how sad and hurt he was when they broke up. He acknowledged that this is one of the prices he will have to pay as an actor:

"I think it's something you have to learn to manage. The sad thing is, sometimes relationships will suffer. It isn't easy to be uprooted from your friends and family constantly, but I love what I'm doing."

After a short vacation in 2001 after wrapping up *Rings*, Orlando went to Los Angeles to meet with producers and directors about new movie roles. Although everyone knew he would be in *The Lord of the Rings*, the first movie had not been released yet, and Orlando was still a new and relatively inexperienced actor. But as it turned out, he was also a lucky one. While in Los Angeles he met with noted director Ridley Scott about a war movie called *Black Hawk Down*. The movie is set in Somalia during 1993, and tells the true story of an American military operation gone wrong. Orlando was cast as Todd Blackburn, a U.S. Army soldier who falls from a helicopter during a battle and breaks his back.

To play Blackburn, Orlando had to learn how to speak with an American accent. He also had to think and act like an American, not an Englishman. The cultural differences between the two countries can be subtle, but Orlando knew that it was important to get them right. In addition to these considerations, all of the actors also took part in military training exercises at Fort Benning in Georgia. They met with Army Rangers and learned what it had really been like during that horrible battle in Mogadishu, Somalia.

Although both movies were about loyalty, teamwork, and fighting for what is right, Orlando found the filming of *Black Hawk Down* to be very different from *The Lord of the Rings*. The *Rings* trilogy had been filmed over a long period of time and every aspect of the project was

In this scene from the 2001 film *Black Hawk Down*, Orlando's character Todd Blackburn is being tended to after falling from a helicopter. The film depicted a battle that occurred during 1993 in Mogadishu, Somalia, when members of a militia commanded by warlord Mohamed Aidid shot down two American helicopters. Eighteen Americans were killed during the battle.

tightly controlled. *Black Hawk Down* was filmed relatively quickly. In order to create the chaotic experience of a battle, director Ridley Scott did his best to keep everyone on their toes. The shoot was disorderly and even violent at times. The actors had paintballs shot at them and were surrounded by the noise and action of Army helicopters. Orlando learned a lot from the experience.

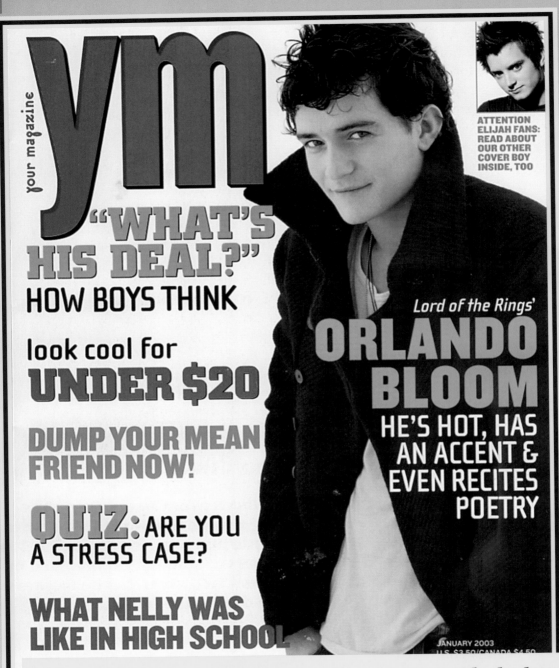

your magazine

ym

"WHAT'S HIS DEAL?"
HOW BOYS THINK

look cool for
UNDER $20

DUMP YOUR MEAN FRIEND NOW!

QUIZ: ARE YOU A STRESS CASE?

WHAT NELLY WAS LIKE IN HIGH SCHOOL

ATTENTION ELIJAH FANS: READ ABOUT OUR OTHER COVER BOY INSIDE, TOO

Lord of the Rings'
ORLANDO BLOOM
HE'S HOT, HAS AN ACCENT & EVEN RECITES POETRY

JANUARY 2003
U.S. $3.50/CANADA $4.50

Because Orlando has great appeal to young people, he has been pictured on the covers of many magazines, including the January 2003 issue of *YM*. The magazine also named him one of its "20 Hottest Guys," and around the same time he was selected as one of *Teen People*'s "25 Hottest Stars Under 25."

Teen Idol

By the time Orlando finished filming *Black Hawk Down*, it was almost time for the first film in the *Rings* trilogy, *The Fellowship of the Ring*, to be released. He joined his costars on a tour to promote the film. They traveled around the world to be photographed and interviewed by reporters, and appeared on television and in magazines. Soon it was hard to go anywhere and not see or read something about *The Lord of the Rings*. Orlando even had his own Legolas action figure at Burger King.

Fans were swept away by Orlando's good looks, and he quickly became a hot teen idol. The public wanted to know everything about him: what his favorite foods were, where he lived, and what he liked to do. The actor received fan mail and requests for autographed pictures.

Orlando was overwhelmed by all the attention. He had not gone into acting to become a teen idol or a sex symbol, but because he liked the challenge of playing different characters. Being photographed every time he appeared in public and having crowds of screaming fans follow him around was more than he had expected. He also worried that if people focused only on his looks, they would not take him seriously as an actor. The number of fan sites on the Internet was especially troubling. Orlando has called himself a **technophobe** and does not have a Web site or even an e-mail address, so the staggering number of fan sites dedicated to him was unnerving. However, he was raised to be a gentleman and has always been polite to his fans.

Being a teen idol also led to **rumors**. After Orlando and actress Kate Beckinsale filmed a commercial together for The Gap, some newspapers ran pictures of them together and claimed they were romantically involved. Orlando had to deny the rumors and tell everyone the truth: he and Kate were just friends and coworkers.

Life was changing fast for the young British actor. He went from nothing to stardom almost instantly, and this was just the beginning. He would be the center of even more attention in the future.

Thanks to the success of *The Fellowship of the Ring*, Orlando found himself in great demand in Hollywood. However, although he was offered many parts, at first he did not find one that he felt was right. He was pleased to take a leading role in the film *Ned Kelly*, about a 19th century Australian outlaw and his gang.

4

Orlando's Big Career

After the success of *The Fellowship of the Ring*, Orlando received many film offers. He quickly discovered, however, that most of the scripts wanted him to play a teen heartthrob. The roles were not demanding, and he knew they would do little to develop new skills and enable him to become a better actor.

A Change of Pace

Instead of taking easy roles, Orlando sought a new challenge in his next movie. He costarred in the film *Ned Kelly*, about a real person who had lived in Australia during the late 1800s. Ned Kelly was like Robin Hood, an **outlaw** who stole from the rich and was beloved by the poor. He is a beloved figure in Australian culture.

When Orlando met with the film's director, Gregor Jordan, he was excited about what he heard. Jordan told him the film would be violent, showing many gunfights between Kelly's gang and the police. But it would also address important themes, such as friendship, loyalty, and honor. In addition, the movie would give Orlando the chance to work with several well-known Australian actors, including Heath Ledger and Naomi Watts. Orlando was cast as Joe Byrne, a friend of Kelly's and a member of his gang.

Orlando studied Byrne's life and the history of the Kelly gang and was fascinated by what he learned. Byrne was a killer and criminal, but he was also well educated, charming, and glamorous. Byrne was the most complex character that Orlando had yet played, and he wanted to portray him accurately and fairly.

Ned Kelly was a far cry from *The Lord of the Rings*. Unlike the *Rings* trilogy, *Ned Kelly* was shot on a very low **budget**. At first it was only released in Australia and Great Britain, where it received poor reviews. The film did not appear in the United States until 2004. In America the film did not do well, and many people did not even hear about it. The failure did not affect Orlando's career, though. He was already preparing for his next feature.

Big Part, Small Movie

Orlando's next movie was *The Calcium Kid*, directed by his friend Alex De Rakoff. This quirky film was a mockumentary, which is a comedy shot in the style of a **documentary**. It told the story of a milkman who became a boxer after drinking so much milk that his bones became incredibly strong. Orlando had the starring role as Jimmy, the milkman. He later admitted that he was glad his first lead role was in a low-budget film, so he did not have the burden of other people's high expectations.

Unfortunately Orlando's first turn as a leading man did not go well. The film was only released in Great Britain. It was trashed by reviewers, who called the film "shamingly bad British comedy," "in desperate need of a backbone," and "too darn sweet." Orlando was also criticized for being "wishy-washy." The film did so poorly that it was removed from theaters after just two weeks. However, Orlando told reporters that he still considered the movie a rewarding personal experience and was glad to have done it.

In *The Calcium Kid* Orlando played the milkman-turned-boxer Jimmy. The low-budget comedy, which was directed by Alex De Rakoff, was released in 2004 in the United Kingdom. *The Calcium Kid* did not do well at the box office, and was never released in American theaters, although in 2005 it was shown on U.S. television.

A Pirate's Life

Even though *Ned Kelly* had been a disappointment at the theaters, it gave Orlando an important industry connection. One of his costars, acclaimed British actor Geoffrey Rush, told Orlando about his next project, a big-budget Disney film called *Pirates of the Caribbean: The Curse of the Black Pearl*. Rush recommended that Orlando read the script. *Pirates* producer Jerry Bruckheimer, who previously had produced *Black Hawk Down*, also wanted Orlando to be involved with the film. He felt the young actor should play the part of blacksmith Will Turner, one of the leading roles.

At first Orlando was not interested in the project. Being a leading man is very different from taking on small character parts that would stretch his abilities. But Geoffrey Rush pushed him to take the part, and Orlando liked the idea of using the sword fighting skills he had developed while filming *The Lord of the Rings*. The tipping point came

Producer Jerry Bruckheimer (right) pauses for a photo with *Pirates of the Caribbean* costars Orlando Bloom (left) and Johnny Depp. Some Disney executives initially questioned Bruckheimer's decision to hire Depp for a leading role in the film. However, it was clear that Bruckheimer had made the right choice when *Curse of the Black Pearl* became a huge international hit.

when Orlando found out that Johnny Depp would play the lead role of Captain Jack Sparrow. Orlando had admired Depp for years and was impressed that this actor, who was known for taking unconventional roles, would be part of the film.

Orlando signed on to play the part of Will Turner, an orphaned blacksmith who is in love with the governor's daughter, Elizabeth Swann. When Will was just a child, the governor and his daughter found him floating among a shipwreck. The two children were good friends from that point on. Over the course of the movie, Will discovers that his father was a pirate, which makes him the only person able to break a curse placed upon the crew of the pirate ship the *Black Pearl*. Orlando described his character this way:

> **"My character, Will, is kind of the earnest young man type, a kind of true blue straight shooter. He's not an obvious pirate. That's part of his arc—discovering that he's from that stock and realizing it's something he needs to come to terms with."**

In order to save Will from the pirates, Elizabeth tells them that she is their dead crewman's child. They take her hostage and head for the cursed treasure so they may finally be set free. Will has no choice but to chase after them to save her, and he finds himself teaming up with Captain Jack Sparrow. While he is no hero, Sparrow offers his assistance because the pirates have something he wants: the *Black Pearl* itself. Eventually, Elizabeth and Will fall in love and Jack gains control of the ship.

A Huge Success

Pirates of the Caribbean: The Curse of the Black Pearl was released in July 2003. Audiences flocked to the movie, sending it straight to number one. The film earned more than $46 million during its opening weekend and $80 million in its first week. By the end of its run, *Pirates* had earned over $300 million in the United States and more than $650 million around the world. Johnny Depp stole the show with his outrageous portrayal of Jack Sparrow, but Orlando's charming and witty portrayal of Will held the film together. Will Turner was a hero that audiences could relate to.

Critics enjoyed the movie and praised Orlando's performance. Mark Sells of the Web site *Film Threat* summed up the reaction to Orlando:

"Offering a perfect counterbalance to Depp's shenanigans are Orlando Bloom and Keira Knightley—two individuals who prove they are stars in the making. . . . These two match Depp's whimsy with wit and humour of their own. It's one of the true pleasures of the film."

In the Spotlight

After *Pirates* was released, Orlando was once again in great demand. Young women lined up for hours to catch a glimpse of him when the

"Will is the straight guy and the dynamic works because Jack Sparrow sparks off Will Turner," explains Orlando. "And you're never quite sure whether Will Turner really understands what Jack Sparrow is talking about, but that's kind of what makes it funny. Because you're laughing at Jack and Will and also with them at the same time."

Orlando and his *Pirates of the Caribbean* costar Keira Knightley are surrounded and photographed by a large crowd. Orlando called the intense public attention that surrounded the 2003 Disney film "a circus." *The Curse of the Black Pearl* was the biggest film of the summer, eventually earning more than $650 million worldwide.

movie premiered, and the air was filled with their screams when he arrived. Orlando was a bit taken aback by all the attention, saying:

"It's just such a circus. . . . I'm trying to adjust to all the changes that are happening. There's mountains of fan mail and it's really a lot to deal with. It's flattering but it doesn't mean anything to me. I'm not interested in being a celebrity or a movie star. I'm just trying to be an actor."

The Orlando-mania intensified when the third *Lord of the Rings* movie, *The Return of the King*, was released later in 2003. Just like the previous movies in the trilogy, *The Return of the King* was very successful. In 2004 it won 11 Academy Awards, including Best Picture. Although Orlando was not nominated for his role as Legolas, he did attend many award shows, which put him even more in the public eye.

The young actor was accompanied to some of these award shows by his new girlfriend, Kate Bosworth. Kate, an actress, had starred in a teen surfing movie called *Blue Crush*. The two had been introduced by a mutual friend in London in 2002 and then reconnected when they met again at the premiere of *The Lord of the Rings: The Two Towers* later that year.

The **media** was very interested in this beautiful young couple, but Orlando and Kate did their best to keep the relationship private. Orlando once told reporters that he felt it was unnecessary to talk about his relationships, although he did admit to a fan that it was tough to date someone when you are always away from home making movies.

A Trojan Prince

Orlando was gaining a reputation for doing costume dramas—movies that featured exotic settings, adventure, and elaborate costumes. In 2004 he signed on to do another one. This time Orlando would play Paris, a Trojan prince, in the movie *Troy*. The film was based on Homer's *Iliad*, one of the great epic poems of ancient Greek literature. According to this legend, Paris had enticed Helen, the most beautiful woman in the world and the wife of a Greek king, to run away with him. This incident began a 10-year conflict known as the Trojan War.

Orlando described his character as immature and impulsive. He had to face his own cowardice in battle. And he was often compared to his brave brother, Hector, the Trojans' greatest warrior. Orlando said the biggest challenge was making a cowardly, selfish character likable, so that the audience would understand what he does and why he does it.

As always, Orlando used his time on the film to learn new skills and observe other actors. Along with technical knowledge, he received an important lesson from the film's star, Brad Pitt. Although Orlando was famous, Pitt was a superstar. When the two went out to dinner one night, Orlando was shocked at the number of people who lined the road, screaming Pitt's name and snapping pictures. Through it all, Pitt kept calm and cheerful, smiling, shaking hands, and always moving

Orlando gets a hug from girlfriend Kate Bosworth, who is also an actor. Kate has appeared in such hits as *The Horse Whisperer*, *Blue Crush*, and *Superman Returns*. Orlando and Kate began dating in 2002. They broke up briefly in 2005, got back together, then broke up for good in the fall of 2006.

In the 2004 film *Troy*, which is loosely based on Homer's epic poem *The Iliad*, Orlando played the Trojan prince Paris, who starts a war between the Greeks and the Trojans by seducing Helen (played by Diane Kruger), the most beautiful woman in the world and the wife of a Greek king. *Troy* eventually earned nearly $500 million worldwide.

forward. His composure impressed Orlando and helped him understand how to cope with his own increasing fame.

Troy was released in May 2004. The exciting story and the film's three handsome male leads brought audiences into the theater but did not impress critics. They complained that the romance between Paris and Helen lacked intensity. If thousands of people were going to die because of that love, critics felt it should have been epic in its passion. Orlando's character was also described as weak and wimpy.

A Different Role

Following *Troy*, Orlando decided he was done with costume dramas. He complained to reporters:

> **"I'd really like to take on a role that doesn't involve a sword. I've had enough of being the cool, clean-shaven Elf; the cool, wholesome pirate slayer. Do I want to be a pin-up? Do I want to just be a poster boy? No, I don't!"**

In November 2003 Orlando made an independent movie set in contemporary times. The film was a crime drama called *Haven*. It was set in the Cayman Islands and told the story of a young man, played by Orlando, who is sucked into a brutal crime by two American businessmen. For the first time, Orlando did not just act in a movie. He was also one of the film's producers.

The young actor enjoyed playing a grittier part that did not feature any heroics. However, the movie received poor reviews when it was released in 2004 and quickly disappeared from theaters. Orlando put the film's disappointment behind him. His career was still going strong.

Orlando is wearing the armor of a knight on the cover of *Ciak*, an Italian magazine. To play Balian, the blacksmith hero of *Kingdom of Heaven*, Orlando had to bulk up. "I put on 15 or 20 pounds," he told *People* magazine. "I've never eaten so much. I had six meals a day, from protein shakes to steak and chicken."

5

Ups and Downs

Although Orlando had previously said he was tired of being cast in costume dramas, that is exactly where his career went next. He took on a starring role in the historical drama *Kingdom of Heaven*. This was the first time Orlando had the leading role in a major motion picture.

Orlando's Kingdom

In 2004 Ridley Scott began shooting *Kingdom of Heaven* in Morocco. Orlando had worked with Scott on *Black Hawk Down* and was eager to work with him again. He also liked the idea of playing a real hero, not a wishy-washy character like Paris in *Troy*.

Kingdom of Heaven is set during the Crusades, a series of wars fought between 1095 and 1291. During this time, Christian soldiers traveled to the Middle East to gain control over the Holy Land—Jerusalem and other places mentioned in the Bible—from Muslim armies that had captured them hundreds of years earlier. Orlando played a blacksmith named Balian who, following the death of his wife and child, questions how God can allow such tragedies. He leaves his home to take part in the Crusades, searching for meaning and redemption. He finds his meaning in defending the innocent and falling in love again.

The part of Balian was a very physical one. Orlando worked hard to get in shape. He put on 20 pounds of muscle and once again used his sword fighting and horseback riding skills on film.

Despite its popular star and a supporting cast of great actors, including Liam Neeson and Jeremy Irons, *Kingdom of Heaven* disappointed audiences and critics when it was released in May 2005. Reviewers felt that Orlando's "pretty boy" image clashed with his portrayal of a brawny hero. Other reviewers complained that despite the film's beautiful scenery, costumes, and action sequences, the experience was boring. The movie's R rating also created a problem, because most of Orlando's teenage fans were too young to see the film.

Another Disappointment

Orlando followed *Kingdom of Heaven* with a very different movie. *Elizabethtown*, directed by Cameron Crowe, is a romantic comedy set in the present day. Once again, Orlando had the starring role. He played Drew Baylor, an American shoe designer whose poor product idea destroys the company he works for. After his father dies, Drew goes home to fulfill his father's last wish. On the journey he meets a flight attendant played by Kirsten Dunst and begins a romance with her that changes his life.

Once again, however, the film was a critical and commercial disappointment. It seemed that audiences did not want to see Orlando as a charming leading man. They wanted to see him as a swashbuckling hero. It was time for Orlando to go back to his pirate days.

Back to the Caribbean

Because *Pirates of the Caribbean: The Curse of the Black Pearl* had been such a great success, Disney had decided to make two more *Pirates* movies and create a trilogy. Like *The Lord of the Rings*, the sequels

In *Time* magazine's review of *Kingdom of Heaven*, Richard Corliss wrote, "Bloom has matured splendidly (the beard helps). He gives Balian heft and winsomeness as a pensive man of action." Although the film was a box-office disappointment, Orlando won a European Film Award for Best Actor, and was nominated for three Teen Choice Awards for his part in *Kingdom*.

would be filmed at the same time, beginning in 2005. The stars from the original cast signed on to **reprise** their roles.

The second film in the trilogy, *Pirates of the Caribbean: Dead Man's Chest*, was released in July 2006. The film was an instant smash. Once again, audiences filled theaters to see Johnny Depp clown around as Jack Sparrow and witness the romance between Will Turner and

Orlando hugs costar Kirsten Dunst in a scene from *Elizabethtown*, a Cameron Crowe film released in 2005. Dunst later spoke with *Teen People* about Orlando, saying: "He is a doll. He's sweet and down-to-earth, and he's such a dork, which I love. He's very spiritual and very Buddhist in the way that he approaches things."

Director Gore Verbinski (second from left) speaks with Orlando (center) during the filming of *Pirates of the Caribbean: Dead Man's Chest*. The 2006 Disney film earned more than $1 billion internationally. A third film in the series, *Pirates of the Caribbean: At World's End*, was another huge hit when it was released in May 2007.

Elizabeth Swann. The movie also introduced new characters and included many outrageous special effects. *Dead Man's Chest* became the top-grossing movie of 2006, earning more than a billion dollars.

Orlando enjoyed returning to his pirate days. He talked about the change in Will's character:

> **❝[Will] goes from being a straight-laced kind of upright stick in the mud to becoming more of a bit of a pirate in this one, thankfully. It was kind of like discovering my inner pirate for the first time in a way.❞**

After making three *Pirates of the Caribbean* films, Orlando says that he probably won't do another: "I've been doing a pirate movie most of my adult life. I'm excited to explore other avenues." However, he has left the door open to a return as Will Turner: "If it were to take shape in another form down the line, who knows?"

99999999

9999999999

Can't Settle Down

By 2006 Orlando was at the peak of his fame. His private life, however, was not as successful. Although he owned a home in London, he was able to spend very little time there. He had filmed movies all over the world, including New Zealand, Australia, Morocco, Spain, the Cayman Islands, and the United States. This jet-set life might be glamorous and exciting, but it made it hard for Orlando to maintain a steady relationship.

The pressure of work led Orlando and Kate Bosworth to break up in 2005 after dating for two years. Both have said that they love each other, but that the difficulties of their long-distance relationship were just too hard to overcome. Although they got back together for a short time, they split up again early in 2006. Since then Orlando has not been linked to any particular woman, although rumors swirled in early 2007 that he was seeing Spanish actress Penelope Cruz. As always, Orlando has avoided sharing the details of his private life with the media.

Since he finished filming the third *Pirates of the Caribbean* movie, which was released in 2007, Orlando has not taken on any major projects. He has spent time with his family and friends in London, and takes care of his dog, a stray he rescued when he was filming in Morocco. Orlando has also taken short vacations and appeared on a few award shows. He struggles to maintain a regular life despite his fame. He said:

"I prefer the simpler things in life. I love just walking the streets, taking my mum and gran out for lunch, going to see a movie, or having dinner with mates."

With his career success to date, it is clear that Orlando Bloom is no ordinary actor. Surely the best is ahead for this intelligent and talented young performer.

1977   Orlando Jonathan Blanchard Bloom is born on January 13 in Canterbury, England.

1981   Harry Bloom dies.

1990   Orlando finds out that his biological father is really Colin Stone, a family friend.

1993   Moves to London to study acting at the National Youth Theatre.

1994   Gets his first professional acting job on the British television show *Casualty*.

1995   Begins studying at the British American Drama Academy.

1997   Appears in his first movie, *Wilde*.

        Enrolls at the Guildhall School of Music and Drama.

1998   Breaks his back in a fall, and requires risky surgery to enable him to walk again.

1999   Chosen to play Legolas in *The Lord of the Rings* trilogy.

        Graduates from Guildhall.

        Appears in the British television drama *Midsomer Murders*.

2001   Appears in *The Lord of the Rings: The Fellowship of the Ring*.

        Appears in *Black Hawk Down*.

2002   Appears in *The Lord of the Rings: The Two Towers*.

        Films *Ned Kelly,* which is critically panned.

        Films *The Calcium Kid,* which is also disliked by the critics.

2003   Appears in *Pirates of the Caribbean: The Curse of the Black Pearl.*

        Appears in *The Lord of the Rings: The Return of the King*.

        Begins dating actress Kate Bosworth.

2004   *The Lord of the Rings: The Return of the King* wins
11 Academy Awards, including Best Picture.

Orlando appears in the movie *Troy*.

Orlando appears in the movie *Haven*.

2005   Orlando lands his first leading role in a major film,
starring in *Kingdom of Heaven*.

Orlando also stars in *Elizabethtown*.

Orlando and girlfriend Kate Bosworth break up, although
they later get back together.

2006   Orlando appears in the top-grossing movie of the year,
Pirates of the Caribbean: Dead Man's Chest.

Orlando and Kate Bosworth break up again.

2007   Orlando appears in *Pirates of the Caribbean: At World's End*.

ACCOMPLISHMENTS & AWARDS

Movies

1997 *Wilde*

2001 *The Lord of the Rings: The Fellowship of the Ring*
Black Hawk Down

2002 *The Lord of the Rings: The Two Towers*

2003 *Pirates of the Caribbean: The Curse of the Black Pearl*
Ned Kelly
The Lord of the Rings: The Return of the King

2004 *The Calcium Kid*
Troy
Haven

2005 *Kingdom of Heaven*
Elizabethtown

2006 *Pirates of the Caribbean: Dead Man's Chest*

2007 *Pirates of the Caribbean: At World's End*

Awards

2002 Empire Awards: Best Debut for *The Lord of the Rings: The Fellowship of the Ring*

MTV Movie Awards: Best Breakthrough Performance for *The Lord of the Rings: The Fellowship of the Ring*

2003 Hollywood Film Festival Awards: Hollywood Breakthrough Award, Male Performer

GQ Men of the Year Awards: Best Film Actor

2004 Screen Actors Guild Awards: Outstanding Performance by a Cast for *The Lord of the Rings: The Return of the King*

MTV Movie Awards: Sexiest Hero

People magazine "50 Most Beautiful" and "Hottest Bachelors"

Teen People magazine "#1 Hottie"

Books

Barnham, Kay. *Orlando Bloom*. Chicago: Raintree Press, 2006.

Boer, Peter. *Orlando Bloom: Shooting to Stardom*. Edmonton, Canada: Icon Press, 2005.

Carlisle, Jonathan. *Orlando: An Unauthorized Biography*. New York: Razorbill, 2004.

Dougherty, Terri. *Orlando Bloom*. San Diego: Lucent Books, 2006.

Kranenburg, Heather. *Lovin' Bloom: The Unauthorized Story of Orlando Bloom*. New York: Ballantine Books, 2004.

Orr, Tamra. *Orlando Bloom*. Hockessin, Delaware: Mitchell Lane Publishers, 2007.

Parfitt, A.C. *Orlando Bloom: The Biography*. London: John Blake Publishing, 2004.

Steele, Robert. *Orlando Bloom: Wherever It May Lead*. London: Plexus Publishing, 2004.

Web Sites

http://movies.about.com/od/piratesofthecaribbean2/a/ piratesob062906.htm

This Web site features an interview with Orlando about the movie *Pirates of the Caribbean: Dead Man's Chest*.

http://www.full-bloom.net

Here is an archive of articles about Orlando as well as up-to-the-minute news about his career.

http://www.imdb.com/name/nm0089217/bio

The Internet Movie Database has a brief biography, quotes, and trivia about Orlando.

http://www.theobfiles.com

This fan site includes many articles and news items about Orlando.

http://www.theonering.net/movie/cast/bloom.html

This Web site features information about the cast and crew of the *Lord of the Rings* trilogy and their experiences making the movies.

GLOSSARY

acclaimed—enthusiastically praised.

agent—a person who represents an actor and seeks jobs for his or her client.

apartheid—a political system in South Africa from 1948 to the early 1990s that segregated blacks and whites, giving greater rights and privileges to white citizens.

audition—an opportunity for an actor to win a role in a play or movie.

budget—a plan for how money is earned and spent.

challenge—something that is hard to do.

documentary—a movie or television program that presents true facts and information, rather than telling a fictional story.

gross—the amount of money earned before expenses are deducted.

industry—an activity or business that many people are involved in.

media—newspapers, magazines, television, and other sources that report news.

mythical—not real, but based on myth; imaginary.

outlaw—a criminal who tries to avoid capture by the law.

reprise—to repeat a performance.

rumor—a generally circulated story or statement that may or may not be true.

technophobe—someone who is afraid of technology.

Tinseltown—a nickname for Hollywood

trilogy—a group or series of three related works, such as books or movies.

page

ABOUT THE AUTHOR

Joanne Mattern has written more than 200 books for children, including biographies of Eminem, Celine Dion, Bernie Mac, Tom Cruise, and many sports stars. She specializes in nonfiction and especially enjoys writing about animals, interesting people, and important historical events. Joanne also works in her local library. She lives in New York with her husband, four children, and three cats.